VOICES FROM AN ISLAND

Other Books by Marguerite Bouvard

Landscape and Exile, 1985.
Journeys Over Water, 1982.
The Intentional Community Movement: Building a New Moral World, 1975.
The Labor Movement in the Common Market Countries, 1972.

VOICES FROM AN ISLAND

Marguerite Bouvard

Breitenbush Books, Inc.
Portland, Oregon

First printing: November 1985

Library of Congress Publication Data

    Bouvard, Marguerite Guzman, 1937–
      Voices from an island.

      I. Title.
    PS3552.0837V6   1985   811'.54   85-3831

ISBN 0-932576-25-7
ISBN 0-932576-26-5 (pbk.)

Breitenbush Books, Inc.
P.O. Box 02137
Portland, OR 97202

Designed by Susan Applegate of Publishers Book Works, Inc.
Title page art by Aileen Calahan.
Cover photograph by Constantine Manos, © 1985

Manufactured in the U.S.A.

"I, You, the River" in *Road Apple Review*; "Waking" in *Poet Lore*; "The Crab Apple Tree" in *Southwest Review*; "The Unfolding," "What the Body Knows" in *Hollow Springs Review*; "An Inland Sea," "I, Odysseus," "Ivo," "Ali," "Requiem" in *Ohio Journal*; "Voices From an Island," "The Pass Above Flumet," "A Woman Turning Pages" in *Green River Review*; "Antigua" in *Whetstone Review*; "Hands," "The Peaks of Otter," "The Vineyard" in *Literary Review*; "Hands," "The Peaks of Otter," also in *Anthology of American Verse–Yearbook of American Poetry*; "Listening to the Grass" in *Xanadu*; "Knees," "Bearing the Cargo," "Farms on the Col des Annes" in *West Branch*; "Ears," "Eyes" in *Seattle Review*; "Strata," "Herta" and "In the Desert Botanical Garden" in *Ploughshares*; "Tree House," "Karel," "The Sum, Not the Fragments of Many Years" in *Greenfield Review*; "Written in Rain," "Bounthavy Vongsy" in *Poems, A Celebration*, an anthology published by the Newton Free Library; "Japanese Tea Hut with Garden," "In Four Acts," "Tea Hut Buffeted by Weather," "Leaving the Hut for the Road Beyond," "Crosswinds" in *Yarrow*; "Tea Ceremony" in *From Mount San Angelo: Stories, Poems and Essays*; "House Made of Wind" in *Ceasura*.

★   ★   ★

Grateful acknowledgement is made to the Virginia Center for the Creative Arts, the MacDowell Colony, and the Ragdale Foundation where many of these poems were written. Special thanks to Sonya Dorman.

TABLE OF CONTENTS

House Made of Wind

Always the rush of wind.
Even when the trees close by are stilled,
I hear the wind tunneling through the woods,
gathering force until the tree tops
send up their green spume

and the forest opens its pages
like a sacred book. I learn the solidity
of light, a pine with its bark stripped down
shining whitely in a dark trail,
and from a cluster of rocks, how weight
sustains weight.

You sit across the table,
your eyes on fire, your words
rushing towards me. Shaken by wind,
we are weight against weight.
But this is how we learn each other,
knife against wood. The wood
allowing. The knife, dazzling, impatient.
We are like branches rushing
into each other. This is how we learn ourselves.

The wind chants through the forest
in many tongues: *sirocco, bora, mistral, monsoon.*
The forest gathers them all in, accepting
their seasons. It needs a thousand lives
to learn them all. Like Father Francis,
pouring over his books of the Dogan,
the African myths, the "organic ways of the Indian."
He says, "There isn't enough time,"
says, "The lilacs loosening their fragrance
into the wind." For him the truth is always first,
as he carves out his journey, plunging deep
into the forest, far from the tables of the powerful.

The wind says the forest is everchanging
and the poet, at the end of a long life,
writes, "The wonder has never ceased."

The Unfolding

If, in the middle of the chapter the plot
becomes invisible
it is only because we once believed

we held the angles.
Now, from behind a grillwork,
we watch the traffic roll by.

The hair on our son's cheek
thickens and the table
where he sits with a dark-eyed girl

is spinning. Plates, cups, spoons flee
yet the boy is still
in the kitchen sleeping over his workbook

and the sister reads under her pillow
with a flashlight.
In the library, grandfather's cane

stands at attention while Franz Josef
reviews his troops.
Ours was a house with windows, a balcony

overlooking the Hudson.
We called out to the horizon, its blazing ships.
But there were distances

that weighed us down.
Not the sea with its shoreline broken
into two languages

or the train pulling out of Le Havre,
but the father setting off for the Bois
alone with his dog.

He had no words, and his sons, great boys
of forty now, choke on silence.
As mother and father, they tend

an empty house. They walk in and out of
the action on their own cues,
or so they believe. The lines we throw

away bloom over and over again as
the still part of us
watches the part that moves.

Listening to the Grass

From my window I watch dried blades
lean in the sun. The grass knows
about houses, about doors,
hands traveling, naked feet.

Birds drift above while
the land shifts and turns in its bed.
The grass knows
the mute chorus of wheels,

how everything moves yet stays still.
It remembers the child passing through,
light as air, the girl,
her colors, her fragments of song.

This is why old men take out
their chairs, their pipes,
why old women lean in doorways.

I, You, the River

1

As I watch the film uncurl with
its dreamed motion,
a warmth enters my skin.
Like the wild mint
I know that time watches
itself in my green pores.

I listen to the blood
moving through my heart,
listen as the old names
gather
and disappear.

This silence I am learning
to shape, as when
a bird calls again and again
stopping each time
to make an interval;
the still center of the house
before the snow begins.

2

A man, the tides
of a man,
rising and falling,
causing things to be moved,
a fierce wind pushing at doors,
or holding the contours
of a child's face.

You follow the dark thread
of your thoughts, night
after night at your work-table
where the film winds
under your careful hand.

3

Perfection, you say (the will
to be tuned, the frames
spliced into place.)

Spirit, I say (the quick pulse
flaming.)

4

To be young
is to sing the one-note song
of the thrush,
say that sadness
is a harbinger of age,
a shadow reaching
into the vein,
see a thinness ahead,
a narrowing of light.

Safe in the twilight
of their theaters, the young
shake their heads,
take note as they watch us
ride the eddies,
the rough sweep
of a river.

The Sum, Not the Fragments of Many Years

When my daughter speaks, I hear
the grandfather she never knew.
At eighteen, she talks of wanderlust.
She has her great-grandmother's arched back,

her reserve dividing the world
into "those one speaks to,
the others," but also the restlessness
of a wanderer, my father,

who walked in and out of my life.
I see him strolling down the Rua Andrade,
hands clasped behind his back,
stopping to chat with every passerby.

He changed countries
the way one changes blazers
for down jackets, then folds them away.
He was like the clouds which pass over

the Mount Blanc; wool batt becoming
herds of bison, a solitary dolphin.
Yet he recognized in strangers
not only their country, but a region,

not only a language, but a dialect.
His granddaughter loves the music
of intonations, the cadences
of tense and conjugation.

She bends over her grammar as if
she were climbing l'Aiguille du Midi,
its peaks luring her
the way Santiago beckoned my father.

When I visited him in Sao Paulo
he put me on a trolley saying
"ride it to the end of the line and back,
watch the people." Evenings

he turned on the radio. "Listen,
let the language take hold."
This man who could never talk to me.

Written in Rain

Rain again.
The grass waits patiently,
trees blurring against the horizon.
When we arrived in Paris, young, unsure,
the sidewalks glittered with rain.
Rain drew the sky around us
while we drove through the boulevards.

What does it matter which road we take.
The landscape changes. Seasons
claim us, the breath
of clouds. But now it is autumn,
the time to speak
of rain,

the stillness before it comes.
The years scattered, our bodies
kneaded by weather,
beached on the same shore.
A tangle of arms, hips, thighs.

Now while we drive through the city,
afternoons slip by
like minutes. We wave goodbye
to the children.
It was only yesterday.
I want to cry out, to hold you.
Now, before the rain
sweeps us away.

The Season's Turning

The piercing call of the phoebe echoes
through the blank February air,
the ground still hard
beneath my feet, the paleness

of earth and sky a given.
But this early herald tells me
that nothing is given.
The children, the years that held us,

tumble in one door and out the other.
At the table, a new silence.
Hearing the phoebe's persistent cry,
I see you for the first time,

the curve of your body.
Our arms overflow with each other.
What does it all mean? you ask.
Your face so close to mine

has deepened. A continent
has been surveyed, a village
with its skyline of trees. We know now,
it was ourselves.

Markings

Seeing you at the wake, the earth's
dark already invading the room,
you, who used to be so angry,

subdued and pale.
I wanted to tell you, love
is always mottled, streaked

with cloudy veins, that once
I stayed up all night,
the whir of moths filling the room,

the music of cicadas in the privet
when suddenly the first bird
called out as if there were no boundaries.

Your father's voice in the hall,
his hand always out of reach,
your eyes refusing to give way

are what you had, the life
you wore, its rough wool grazing
your cheek. The dailiness of rooms

crowded while you tunneled
deeper into your life
forgetting the wild spaces,

the stark beauty of mountains
seen from miles away.
This will be your landscape:

not only as you dreamed, clean rooms,
smoothed cushions on the sofa,
but the cool weather of slopes

where you climb without markers,
the air of your solitude mingling
with your father's breath.

The Forest

The Woods

The woods' dark interior
is like a mirror at a county fair.
I waver out of proportion
too close for ease or evanescent.
Even the measured
thud of my feet, the rhythm
within my breast cannot shelter.

Around a bend, painted trilliums,
surprising among the column of trees,
the pine's fragrant bark.
They will vanish with the first chill,
become the soft skin of earth I walk on.

The lady slippers are a flock
of swans. I enter the lavender
of distant hills, the sky's edge
melting on a brilliant day.
As I draw close, the nuances of tone
and complexion bewilder, this rich dissonance
in the common air we breathe.

Sigrid

What keeps her toiling through the day
inch by inch with arthritic knees
hands frozen shut? Two or three hours
to get up in the morning,
then it's afternoon. When I curve
into her driveway she is waiting,
thin shoulders, face puffy with cortisone.

Is it her garden's changing colors,
the milk glass and copper
in her living room, a Swedish landscape
from a family long gone?

I watch with her through the months.
Her body's torment
has its own language, its own
laws. It is a country she did not choose.

We talk of painted trilliums, birds.
I am the visitor flushed with news.
She gives me her eyes,
what she knows of completion.

The Children

I am everything to them, the sky's
blue mantle, the sun
bending over a field of lupine
applauding when a breeze
stirs the petals. I never tire
of this dance. Then suddenly
I am earthbound, remembering
the Utah monoliths, isolate, yet visible
from the road's long winding.

Like the time outside an alpine inn,
the scrape of gravel
in the still mountain air.
I heard my laughter, weightless
in the far future, a breeze
in my son's remembering.

Or the morning I lay in bed, alone
in the first light, staring at the wall.
Then faintly, the wind's dizzying passage.

The Exiles

Ivo

Seated over a glass of slivovitz,
you tell me how the Allies turned you over
to Tito's Partisans, you,
a Croat officer.

Marching through the woods
in front of a rifle,
roots catching at your feet
you prayed only that your mother

would find the burial place.
You pause, listening
to the hollow thud of boots
remembering how one evening

your guard stole a piece of bread,
and pressed it into your manacled hands.
Partisan, Ustaschi.
There are no ideas, only men.

Karel

In the city you miss the trees.
In New Hampshire with only the birches,
you miss the traffic.

The shadows under your eyes
are dark wells. You carry them
from city to city, on tour

with your guitar. Sometimes your face
is all shadow. You remember
campaigns against *bourgeois decadence*,

the banning of songs, and in '69,
the flight from Prague. In Munich
you have a room, an address.

Home is Kromeriz,
but the borders move;
the language of your brothers changes.

Moravia lives in the peasant's
song, *God who gives us
hunger, give us also bread.*

  Ali

In Teheran, the streets overflow
their banks. Rows of clenched fists
crowd the television screen.
What are they looking for,

something to stand on, the names
of fathers, or the present
coiled like a spring in a rifle's
throat? Books, newspapers,

telephone wires tumble down.
But the streets are blind and deaf,
have no desires. In New York City, Ali,
you keep silent. You have brothers.

Nights, in your room, you read
Nietzsche, *to understand the other side.*
Within each of us, you say, *lie the roots
of light, the pull towards dark.*

The Weight of the World

Now the landscape unfolds inside.
We used to watch it and shake our heads.
We could walk away then.

We thought we had moorings, fathers,
precincts we could slip
in and out of.

While we slept they all moved,
the roads smelling of fresh asphalt,
breakers pounding against the shore

with their harvest of broken planks,
and the faces yelling
in Creole on the television screen.

We can't modulate the colors or sounds.
They cling to us, hold
the odor and shape of our clothes.

Listen, this is what roots me,
a mulch of pine needles
in the forest,

a spider's thread stretched across
the window, so fragile
even my breath stirs it.

And the names have moved.
We can no longer pluck them,
say, *this garden, this tree is mine,*

you with no surname
baptized by a slave master.

When you close your eyes,
the Port-au-Prince market lives,
spices, aromas, the night jasmine.

You are the village woman
balancing her water jug.

The Farms on the Col des Annes

After a storm, the grass
springs back, the meadow simmering;
gentian, buttercup, chervil,
cinquefoil. The bees mutter.

Here where mountains rush into clouds
is our beginning, the wood shingles
on the roof held down by stones.
From the heart of the farmhouse

with its kerosene lamps,
its scents of dung and hay,
we climb into the stars,
the animals' steady breathing

ferrying us through darkness.
But on the slope above, derricks
loom in the middle of pastures.
The ski-lift sinks its teeth

into our roots, the gouged earth
bleeding. Throughout the shadowy folds
of the mountains, the farmers
dream of stilled plows.

Bearing the Cargo

1

Travel lightly. But
my head buzzes with passengers.
There's a quarrel inside,
someone scribbling
letters.
I'm a speck on the road
surrounded by a cloud of insects.

As the road lengthens, I use it
to measure, giving speeches
on weathering.
In my pockets are manuals
on stress, seams and paving.
The road sways under me.
Sometimes I am crazy with dust.

Days whirl by. Something
is always missing,
rain for the desert, sirocco
to blow away mist. Choose
we say, but who draws the lots
which send this one
to prison, that one to the beach?

2

My house has no locks.
Nights, visitors can enter
unannounced. A woman appears
in my room with her sun-
parched village.
Wrapped in black she stands
grieving.

Behind me, someone
is cutting a swath through
the foliage. When I wake,
the wilderness fades.

3

Shivering outside the oak door,
I study the details, plot
my assault. First the hinges.
I try to corrode them
with tears, try boring holes,
finding a loose plank. I sing
hymns to it, beat it
with my fists.
When my skin begins to heal
I notice the threshold.

Hands in my pockets I stroll
down a boulevard spacious as the
Avenida Chapultepec with its
green islands, its red
and yellow flags. A clear autumn
light washes the buildings.
The dust is gone.

The Vineyard

In Burgundy, the vineyards are laid out
over centuries, from father
to son in a patchwork of terraces.

The soil gathers in hail and drought,
and as it shifts under the rain,
gives off odors of raspberry

or fox, the aroma in glasses of
Ladoix where two brothers
sit over dinner. One sees

espaliered trees hugging the walls
of an old house. The other
circles the California fields

like a red-tailed hawk. He trains
his roots for far-flung paths.
His brother plants vines

with deep and narrow roots, seeking
nourishment among stones.
They sit down with lives they cannot tell,

the same grape, the same seed,
only their shadows brushing
on the white expanse of the table.

Antigua

The sea has its foliage,
blue-green algae, deep amethyst
of coral. But the island
is a bone. Caribs and Arawaks
have melted back into the earth

taking a landscape, its seasons,
birds flickering among eucalyptus.
Now, only the raw earth,
a country of dust, corrugated roofs
under the hot eye.

Sugarcane and goats ripple
across the fields. In Yuroba villages
the old gods move
like wind through savannahs.
Now the shoreline blooms

green and white umbrellas,
the sand neatly raked, the debris
swept away. No more pirate ships
entering the bay, blood
trickling from dark fountains.

Today the body rustles
in blue and white uniforms.
At the mouth of the bay,
limestone cliffs hold the horizon
like calipers.

Mornings a curve of pure onyx
is silhouetted against the rocks.
A man with white hair
balances an oar, walks
as if he were wearing the sky.

I, Odysseus

In her room, Penelope
unravels tapestry,
trusting in thread which slips
through shuttles, in the tides.

She is faithful, if to be fixed
like the white rock at Duino, mute
among the waves' rustle,
is faithfulness.

But I am Odysseus, married
to the road's labors,
given to hallucinations.
I remember the sirens,

how blue glimmers of song
sent tremors through my skiff.
I even lost my bearings.
But who's to say I was less constant

than one who never let the wind
try her canvas. In my travels
I learned that interludes
on flower infested islands

are a form of death, that life
is the dour music of waves.
As for the visions, the cyclops
still invades my sleep,

his features rooted
in the landscape. Listen,
it's not the sails flapping,
but what hoists them,

the need to whittle space,
to take it head on,
my heart journeying toward her
like a wild bird.

Voices from an Island

Thera 1500 B.C.

An odor of sea
penetrates the hills.
In the houses
there is a rattle of cups.

The air is rich
with sage. On the frescoes
lilies red as the sun enter
the wind while a young woman
bends over them.

At noon in the square
the stony trot of donkeys
echoes. Women
slap linen against the fountain.

In the dark heart of the mill house,
men measure out barley.
Deaf to the fishmongers' cries,
the tumble of children,
they hear only the flick
of grain in the pan.

Theran Girl Resettled in Syracuse

At night when I am home
again, the land rises up
to smother me,
the earth I tilled with
my own flesh.

It surged toward me
sending rocks
in my face, houses
sliding downward.
Half-blinded,
I watched the land plunge back
into the sea.

One morning,
the island was swathed
in pale light,
the barley hushed, the air
motionless. Then,
a drone of wasps.

A new land.
How to gather in?
At first
I tried to forget, thought
that if I emptied myself
the grief would drain away.

There are new streets now,
new foliage.
The birds here have their own
songs.

Days turn. A voice wells up
again, an echo.
Then, trees lift the tips of
their branches.
Houses have faces
I can take between my hands.

Theran Farmer, 1975

In spring
when I walk behind my horse,
bands of earth
widen into daylight,
shards appear
between the barley's pale shoots.

One afternoon
as I followed my animals
into a cave, a goat
stepped through the floor.
I saw a staircase
winding below, then
the broken lines of streets,
thresholds.

Houses speak when
they are empty. An odor
lingers. The floors know
the old footfalls, the hands
that scrubbed them.

We plane down
the swollen boards on doors,
calk windows,
believing we own our houses.

An Inland Sea

In the country I left, I tended
the sky, a tangle of grass
outside my window.

Always I woke up new
to a morning with roads,
the particular shine

of clay,
a clean sweep of fields.
My room had no roof. Hawks

rode the currents above
and I drifted
with the land,

turning and unfolding like the ocean.
It was vast, yet
intimate,

a shelter with doors
that kept opening.
In the country I left behind

my house was transparent, a clear
bowl. I was the water
changing shape

or lying motionless
so that clouds could
swim through me.

Requiem

for the Mhung people

With the slow cadence of branches,
the headman lifts his reed pipe.
As he bows, years unfurl
in the throats of grandfathers,

the gait of women in bright plumage,
measuring the seasons,
note by note, a long trek
across China from a land

of mountains and sparse light.
He dances and the forest
contains its mysteries.
His highland, his village

with its rice fields
is the cloth, the clan a thread.
Across the ocean
in a windowless room

men are tapping their pencils,
while their proxy hunts,
his plane dropping bags
of poisoned rice.

From the cockpit, the pilot sees nothing.
Only the blur of motors,
the miniature dials of the panel.
He could be crop dusting

in Kansas, one more turn then home
as his country's flag
keeps vanishing. He is
the sorcerer, waving his quartz clock

over centuries, green fields.
In the villages, faces
peel like bark. Even the trees
shrink back into their roots.

The English Lesson

Holding out a cup of tea
you say,

tsiao nam sah.
The bird in your throat

rustles.
But you stumble

over *Thursday*.
We discover that

changes in weather
hurl us through

space
like astronauts.

Water won't pour.
Syllables

catch on the tongue.
Weightless,

we reach for rice bowls.
Lamps, clocks,

mirrors elude us.
In outer space,

to walk is
to labor. Docked,

we will pick our way
across lava flows,

lunar rocks,
both of us moonwalkers.

Bounthavy Vongsy in Needham, MA

Arms folded,
you lean in the doorway

of your new house,
light

as a cluster of leaves.
In your eyes

is more time
than I will ever know

though I chase it
with scissors.

Beside you,
the four-year-old child

with an infant's body,
the transparency

of the very old.
You do not complain,

you greet me with a bow,
palms joined

above the forehead.
I bend towards you

stiff-waisted.
I know now,

the forehead is sacred,
hears God

in syllables of rain,
the slow unfolding

of fields.
I want to reach over.

But across the Mekong
is still another river.

In the Desert Botanical Garden

At first they repel me, the octopus
cactus with its spines,
the hedgehog cactus, cane cholla,
prickly pear.

Ungainly like the organ pipe plant,
they hug the ground
with their wooly heads, their ribs
seamed with barbed wire.

But lacking grace, they are graceful,
like Wei Fei the archer
who in his old age pierced eagles
without lifting his bow,

the power lying in what he withheld.
Walking among this wild
profusion of shapes,
I am swept into a grand ball,

the dancers stunned
beneath so much radiance;
James, whose father never touched
his hand, Elaine

lifted from the mangled car
who never again heard
her son's voice
or wakened ear deep in bird song.

One by one we face each other,
without apologies
or explanations. I learn
the harsh beauty of deprivation,

how in chill weather,
the prickly pear deepens
to purple, the crucifixion thorn
turns green.

Strata

The skin we didn't ask for, the skin
of weather keeps us shivering
in Gorky. The question

is whether to greet it
like the Afghan peasant walking
barefoot through snow

or open an umbrella,
take a crash course in camouflage,
learn to ski.

The skin of place which wears
the landscape, glows
with an Asian afternoon,

the musical shine of melons.
Among millet fields and baobab
it gathers in the night.

The skin we wear alone chafes.
All our years we wrestle
like Michaelangelo's *Bound Slave*.

In the heart of our motion,
the skin begins to resonate. It speaks
and the ground falls away.

What the Body Knows

Begin with feet. They know the solidity
of rooms, doorways, stairs
of different heights.

They have their memories, the silk
of grass, ice glazing the culverts,
autumn leaves.

The stomach is an aviator
spinning through galactic space,
shifting altitudes

abruptly.
It can be eloquent, a fire glowing,
a furnace stoking

the body.
As for the lungs, they know when
to hold, when to let go.

Mouths have seasons of milk, sap
and earth.
They are wind harps, river banks

telling us nothing about air or water
how they continue
after the body closes.

Eyes

Eyes have their seasons.
First we see an outline, fragments
of a hand,

columns of light falling through windows.
Then we take a star-shaped
leaf and say hawthorne.

But soon the eyes gear themselves
like clocks.
They parcel the landscape,

become so remote
clouds turn without them,
the sky vanishes.

In autumn, contours reappear,
a foliage of shadows.
Sorrow sharpens the eyes.

They learn to fly out between the lids,
find themselves in other faces.
Like swallows, they nest

in cathedrals and old buildings,
invent gardens,
trees along sandy roads.

Hands

Hands are not blinded. They know
that what fits in the palm,
say a stone or a shell

becomes vast as a city.
Hands are what we need to journey,
fresh water springs

for the thirsty,
tents to shield the head from weather.
Without words, they tell us

what we want to hear. When they join
around a table they are a river
rising above its banks.

Poised in mid-air, the hands
want to believe,
hold a bird or a feather.

While we sleep, they stretch out into
the towns of our childhood,
gather an odor of leaves and rain.

Ears

Ears are tethered to their precincts,
draw the wind's
syllables through poplars,

cypress or baobab.
They decode the tricks weather
plays with our voices,

turbulence in the upper air,
atmospheric conditions
in the dim crevasses of the skull.

When frequencies
are jammed by enemy satellites,
ears put on a skin of anger,

raise their scissors.
The air becomes impassable.
Alone in the woods,

ears follow water among stones,
the soft drum beats of grass.
Nights, they pluck invisible strings.

Knees

Though knees roost on stone floors
or cushions of dust,
they have climbed mountains,

heard rivers rustling underground.
Like fledglings, knees
must leave their perches,

fly over tall grass.
Sometimes they thrust themselves forward
like rebel's fists

or they want to hide
their awkwardness from strangers.
In foul weather

eyes are quick to lose moisture;
but knees cannot lay down
their burdens.

When heaviest,
they feel a tremor, discover
they are part of

a single wave which flares
and continues.
They learn to skate,

to show bravado, bending
and pushing
as the body glides over ice.

A Woman Turning Pages

Mornings, the foreground
fills her room.
She memorizes the walls,
each door, the play
of light on geraniums.

But it's the rain which calls
her, sends her trekking
into the mountains among
stones, swirls of cloudy water.
She hurries through the blurred landscape

with only the air to hold her.
Then, as she looks in the mirror,
maples burn red and yellow.
A tapestry of fields
curves behind her shoulder.

Nights, she sails off with
the shutters flung wide. Walls,
houses, fences melt.
Everywhere the rustle of water.
And she, the riverbed.

Tree House

When I open the door I greet
myself.
I'm transparent here

like the stream flowing under
these branches,
its surface mottled by wind,

its ribs clogged with shoes.
Mornings
my eyes go fishing, browse

among fields, blades of grass.
The real alchemists,
they multiply bright fish.

My arms are still as a forest
and have no borders.
They say, *take this green leaf*

between forefinger and thumb.
It's a lesson the hands
won't forget even when snow

marks out a space somewhere.
In the center, my school desk.
I bring my footsteps here,

try to read their dust.
That staff in the corner, the lemon tree,
is my mother's voice.

The Crab Apple Tree

This anarchy of limbs filling
my window, each finding its shape.
Raw will and the fine
calligraphy of nerves at the tips.

A life, more than the sum
of defeats, the years of siege
in the walls of your self.
More than the resolutions,

the occasional mercies when
you smoke your pipe
and the aroma warms you,
the breath of friends.

Caesuras in which the gulls
drain from your hands
and clean pages show through.
A life, allowing others.

The shape, a constellation
of curves, the half-finished
gestures mingling and the topmost
branch, a pure solitary note.

Okefenokee

What looks solid
through the telephoto lens,
canopies of branches, an archipelago,

is unpredictable as flesh.
Indians named these islands
shaking earth.

White-tailed deer feed
in the underbrush.
On the oak and sweet gum

Spanish moss spreads like a galleon
over tea-colored water.
Nothing here is immobile.

The Sewanee pushes its way
in slow cadence, bass drifting
in its channels.

Always the marsh resists. Swampers
close their doors at dusk.
The loggers' half-finished gestures,

the carefully laid railroad ties
are forgotten. Here, beauty
unfolds in a puzzle.

The August heat erupts
in brush fires, simmering
for months. Then, the quelling hands

of autumn rains. Ponds
fill the charred craters.
The wilderness plunges into itself.

Waking

Outside your hospital window
the trees have thinned
baring a skyscraper,
the gridiron of a highway.
Here cars swing by

flowing into Back Bay
past the bow window where
you leaned as a child,
watching the rain-soaked
poplar inch closer.

You wait, surprised
like Jonah, the walls
around you slippery,
netted with veins,
the ocean surging

with its streamers of fish,
its flecked waves.
For days, an empty laundry
cart has rumbled
past your door.

What time is it? you ask,
wishing for home, the basement
room where you open
your Bible, light
candles for a friend.

After the Elegy

For my mother

A stranger occupies the space
beside me at Mass.

But if the Adriatic whispers
when I'm in Cambridge,
your breath fills my lungs.

Your hands are the language
I lapse into.
They were pontoons for our

difficult crossings.
They dreamed pale shoots,
a country of salvias.

   *

In Senegal the dancers wave masks
so their dead
can slip inside,

wear a skin of earth again.
They whirl together
the years pausing.

I invent my own rituals,
sending letters across
the water,

riding Charon's bow.
But the air can't hold you.

Mary

"She's stubborn," your sister would say,
"She won't see the doctor, won't
even try to get well."

But you were just bored. For weeks
you never left the apartment.
The rows of plants on the windowsill,

meals to prepare couldn't hold you.
Outside, the city churned;
muggers in the park,

headlines crowding the television.
You didn't know
what it was all coming to.

Nights, when the sleep wouldn't come,
you had time to journey back:
all those years in the family

you were everybody's hands.
They never knew what you were thinking.
Finally, you held the reins. No one

could stop you from reaching
for your prize. It was what you claimed
for yourself, this death.

Memorial

Shall we hold a ceremony for absence?
It is a pool of stillness
in the heart of a busy street,

a walkway without footsteps,
a blank door. You notice it more
than you notice

the woman sleeping by your side,
the wilderness of skin
and limbs which gives your own body

corridors and windows. You feel it
more than you feel
the morning enter your room

with its blue wings, its squares
of light on the windowsill.
Presences circle us

like faithful dogs, waiting
for a caress, the acknowledgement
in our voices. But absence

arrives without warning and
is always mistimed.
Take the flower bed next door;

day lilies, sweet william, salvias
cascading under the July sun
just when their gardener has died.

Herta

In the hushed time before
everyone awakes and your hands
enter the day with their

ceaseless journey between table and sink,
you muse over coffee, your own self
rising like a flame.

Your hands are the laths and beams
of the house with its corridors,
its marble steps threading

so many stories; the top floor
with its roof terrace where your son
took to his books,

the floor with rows of empty rooms,
and just below, the one
with rooms of heavy furniture.

Your room is the smallest, only a cot
and a door opening onto a balcony,
"your garden," coleus

croton, a fledgling pine.
The yard below is smothered
under magnolia and vines, a dark tangle

of leaves where your husband passes
like a shadow. Thirty-two years
in the cavernous dusk

of the house. You stayed. Only
a morning swim for yourself
in the long Rimini beaches,

the waves brushing your body,
the old griefs ebbing away.
You breast stroke

like the younger Herta in Trieste,
"so beautiful, even the stones
turned over."

Crosswinds

Once I woke with a start.
During my absence, winter
will seize my village.
When I open the door,
my hut will be empty. Even the cat,
the rags of dark under the table,
will vanish. The garden will be just
a patch of earth, and the shadows
conjugations of brush.

On the road I was lured
by noises, by that other landscape
where we dream of knowing.
What I couldn't reach
was made beautiful by longing.

Perhaps I was lost. Inside me
the heaviness of walls, chasms
between outstretched hands.
I entered the woods,
letting the stillness engulf me.

If we could be like this,
the air rinsed,
cardinals flashing among branches.
If we could be with each other
as bird, tree, air.

The Peaks of Otter

for Helen

The mountains keep opening their blue
doors as we curve among miles
of oak forest, two friends

telling their lives, the countries
they left behind. "Only this is real,"
you murmur as the slopes

rise and fall. But the earth
has reflections deeper than water.
They pull me back,

the old events whispering around me
like wheels against pavement.
They hold me as we drive

higher and higher past fresh snow,
sheets of ice clinging to rock.
When we reach the peaks,

a late afternoon sun zigzags across
the lake; black ice, reeds
pooled in light. On this shore

the web of years shatters
then dissolves, the mountain rises
above us like pure thought.

The Pass Above Flumet

Nights the cowherd's hut
is a lantern.
Soon the pass will be bedded
in autumn snows.

Valleys unravel below us,
flocks of birds.
The peaks are steeped
in shadow,

dark blue rimmed with gray.
So much space.
We have lost the names
of weeks, holidays,

the journey that brought us here.
The particular swing
of our stride
is even as breath.

On the Col des Deux Annes
summer pastures are ribbed
by hooves, grass tufts
shined by so many tongues.

We too have tasted the mountain.
Its smell clings to our shoulders.
Liquor from the roots
of gentians leaves its silt

in our throats.
Our children and our childrens'
children write us letters,
a cure for cancer,

the birth of a girl,
a car skidding on ice.
Now, we can almost
touch the peaks.

In Four Acts

In the mountains, light is center stage,
lemon or silver among the aspens,
fields of bittersweet.
Though I walk for miles,
the hours are motionless.
I am neither farther nor closer.
I am aspen, bittersweet,
the river's eye.

But when I walk through streets,
I am divided; pushed towards,
driven away. Faces eddy around me,
and I, in a darkened theater
as the No Drama glides by. The masks
are gods, warriors, devils
yowling their notes or chanting
their loneliness like reeds
cut off at the roots.

In the intervals between the clack
of sticks, I hear the drumbeat
of plants, the music of limbs
as the body enters sleep.

In the silence beneath our words
I hear the systole and diastole
humming. It tells me that we fear
colors we cannot name, the tenderness
that draws us beyond our edges.

Japanese Tea Hut with Garden

The rocks are placed on bare ground.
They are partly submerged,
rooted in earth. As I gaze at them
the earth vibrates like guitar strings,
faster and faster until
the rocks ripple like water.

In this landscape—pale sky
above a weathered hut and the last smears
of light descending, lavender,
apricot, lemon—are both wolf and deer,
white tails flashing among trees,
shadows assembling.

*

Beyond the hedges, fields surge
towards the horizon
like the movements of a symphony.

But the music that rises
in this rectangle of earth is more beautiful,
the fierce whispering of grass,
continuous as the shuush of waves:
we, changing places around the table,
my son where once my mother sat
surrounded by children and grandchildren.
Shuush, shuush, as we melt into each other.

The twang and clatter of stubble,
our bodies moaning
under the weight of lovers,
of houses, their gutters cracking
from the accumulation of ice and leaves.

*

The weather's in my eyes,
afternoon dissolving into rain,
a brilliant confusion of leaves, red,
cranberry, orange, like children
tumbling through a schoolyard,
then snow whirling around the hut.

All this cancelled before
rocks in their caesura of earth,
the tones muted, browns melting into mauve.
It could be March,
the time before leaves or flowers,
before the earth loosens.

The hut with its doors flung wide
is Wabi, the poverty of heart
whose music is rain,
the crunch of gravel on the walk.
The bare branches are like fishnets
against the horizon.
The sky is reined in by an arc of birds.

Tea Ceremony

Through the doorway, the pared earth,
fishbone trees and shadows
scattered like ornamental rocks,
a garden serene as the Ryoan-ji in Kyoto,
and the sky an unplowed field.

It tells me that the days I herd
like an animal trainer, urging
each hour onto its chair,
cannot be driven,

that I must follow the hours
moving across the lawn
like stately beasts.

It tells me that a simple room,
a table for writing, a cot, a few chairs,
leaves space for the ochres
and purples of the heart.

In this room, I draw up a straight-
backed chair for my grandmother.
I sit by the bedside
of my aunt dying in Rimini.

We don't need to speak, our thoughts
the fragrances of green tea.

Tea Hut Buffeted by Weather

The earth's still damp from yesterday,
rain pooled in ditches,
silver-gray drops clinging
to branches. But the sky opens,
heavy clouds crossing
like freight trains.
Sea winds invade the garden
and the herring gulls scream
until windows shake
and the walls tremble with desire.

★

The cat paces before my door,
yowling for milk,
a leg to rub against.
In the distance, a train
hoots and rumbles and in my hut,
voices: one screams for applause,
two are quarreling over dice
while another rails at the dark.
I settle on my tatami, a fisherwoman
waiting for the splash rings
to close inward.

★

In the rain, tones heighten
as if freshly laid; rust,
tobacco, corn-silk yellow. No hint
of distances, odors of sea.
The road beyond is clear
of trucks, yapping dogs.
There is only the rain, soft, steady,
wrapping me in meditation.

Leaving the Hut for the Road Beyond

I take a back road, winding through fields,
a scattering of houses.
Always I carry my garden, its rivers
of shadow, clouds billowing above the roof,
though sometimes what is closest
is hard to see.

This morning the red clay shines,
the rosemallow nods in the wind.
When I pass the oak, its gnarled limbs
radiate outward.
I bow in recognition.

★

At the bend dogs leap around me
snarling at my heels.
They have a system. They want to control
the road, want me to genuflect.
"It's for your own good," they bark.
I see the panic behind their eyes.
I mean to pass.

★

When I meet pilgrims, we seldom speak,
each intent on his own journey.
Sometimes we share a stump, a cup of tea,
words simple as bread.
In my travels I have learned
how the body prays, each gesture
containing its opposite: the lame man
running with elands,
the one bent under invisible weights
unfolding wings.

★

I carry a friend's letter.
He wants me to bring him my story.
I cannot tell him that I travel this road
as if I were a bird answering
the slant of light, a pattern of stars.
Each morning I unroll my mat
with trepidation, enter a room
of shadows and strange voices.

Friend, the journey has its price:
to leave your house,
your coat, your shoes. Let the wind
knead flesh and bones
until they become doors.